Sailing is one of the most enjoyable and challenging sports in the world. It is a sport that everyone can take part in whether you are 8 years old or 80 years old with boats for all abilities and budgets too.

The RYA National Sailing Scheme is the world's leading small boat sailing scheme with over 80,000 people annually taking part in one of the many courses which make up this accessible and affordable training scheme.

The RYA Advanced Sailing Handbook has been produced to accompany the five advanced sailing modules within the National Sailing Scheme and follows on from the first book in the series, the Start Sailing Handbook.

The National Sailing Scheme training courses can be followed in a variety of boats from dinghies, to keelboats, to multihulls and whilst some techniques and manoeuvres are generic, others are more boat specific and this publication explains and helps you understand these advanced techniques.

So whatever your choice of boat you can be assured that by following an RYA training course you will be taking part in a tried and tested programme designed to help you maximise your progress and develop effective and safe sailing skills.

With over 750 RYA Recognised Training Centres worldwide you will have lots of places to choose from for training, all of which undergo a rigorous annual inspection to ensure that you undertake your training course in a safe and well equipped venue under the guidance of trained and experienced RYA instructors.

Hope you enjoy the book and happy sailing.

John Thorn
RYA National Sailing Coach

 Available on DVD (with this publication) where you see this symbol.

The RYA is committed to encouraging both women and men to participate in sailing.
For clarity only, this book is written using the masculine gender e.g. man overboard.

1 | Seamanship Skills

To carry out any of the manoeuvres in this section, follow these easy steps:

PREPARATION   Take a moment to ensure that you, your crew and equipment are fully prepared.

COMMUNICATION   Discuss plans and how best to execute them, with your crew.

APPROACH   Approach so that the manoeuvre is as simple as possible. If you need to stop, what force will stop you? If you need to turn, what will help you turn?

EXECUTION   Complete a smooth, effective manoeuvre with an escape plan for misjudgement or unforeseen situations.

Seamanship can be defined as 'the easy way' to complete a manoeuvre.

Launching and Recovery

Launching from a **Windward** Shore (Wind Blows off the Shore)

Rig the boat and hoist sails ashore, bow pointing into the wind. Attach the rudder if the blade can be held up.

Ensure sheets run free and launch with the bow into wind, stern first.

The crew holds the boat in water deep enough for the helm to prepare the rudder. If your boat has a **dagger board**, set it down far enough for the boom to clear the top of it.

When the area to **leeward** is clear, the crew pushes the bow off and climbs in. The helm **backs** the jib to turn the bow away from the shore.

The wind will take you away from the shore making for a simple departure.

Before fully sheeting sails in, set the rudder and centreboard.

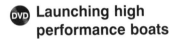 Launching high performance boats

Fully battened sails are harder to de-power, so to maintain control:

- Hoist sails just before launching.
- Leave sail controls slack as the boat is launched (kicker, cunningham).
- On return, drop the mainsail immediately.

Dinghies with little inherent stability and **fully battened** sails will be easier to control afloat if the crew boards first, balancing the boat whilst setting the centreboard and jib. The helm pushes the boat off, climbing aboard over the stern or the side, with wind pressure on the sails providing stability.

Catamarans are sometimes better launched with the rudders and dagger boards raised, sails flapping and crew hanging on the bow to act as a sea anchor. The cat stays head to wind and drifts out before lowering rudders and sailing away.

Step 1

Step 2

Returning to a Windward Shore

Step 1 Sail toward the landing area on a close reach, taking account of the tidal flow and leeway as the board is raised.

Raise the centreboard a little and release the rudder hold down mechanism, partially raising the rudder if necessary.

Let the jib fly or furl it.

Step 2 Sail slowly towards the shore with the mainsail partially flapping.

Control boat speed with the main sheet. Ease fully as you reach the shore.

Step 3 Before the boat touches the shore the crew raises the centre board and exits to windward to take hold of the bow. Make holding the boat easier by dropping the mainsail as soon as possible after landing.

TOP TIP

Control boat speed by holding the main-sheet falls together, rather than pulling metres of sheet through the blocks.

Step 3

DVD Launching from a Lee Shore (Wind on to the Shore)

With the wind blowing onto the shore there are additional considerations.

- Hoist the jib on shore. Launch and turn the boat head to wind with the crew holding the boat in water deep enough to keep it from hitting the bottom.

- The helm can now hoist the main, either from shallow water beside the boat or aboard.

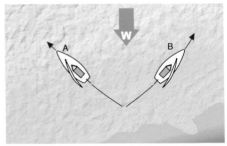

Choice of tack is important because the wind direction is rarely directly onshore

As you hold the boat head to wind, note the angle relative to the shore. If the port side of the boat is nearer the shore, leave on port tack. If the starboard side, leave on starboard tack.

- With your preferred tack chosen, check the centreboard and rudder are down as far as possible, and the sailing area is clear.

- The crew gives a firm push into deeper water and climbs in as the helm sets the rudder and sheets in the mainsail.

- The crew lowers the centreboard fully and sets the jib.

Bow first launching from a lee shore

Boats with fully battened sails and little inherent stability, or those launching into waves will not be able to hoist sails afloat:

Hoist sails ashore and launch the boat bow first. This presents the 'V' section to the waves.

Move the boat into deep water quickly so it does not drop off a wave onto the trolley. If the beach shelves gradually, carry the boat in. Ensure you have enough carriers to avoid a back injury.

Depart using the same considerations for the preferred tack, with crew on board first.

🅾 Returning to a Lee Shore

> **GOLDEN RULE**
> Make sure you can stop. With the wind astern, easing the sheets will not de-power the sail. Reduce sail area to slow the boat.

Step 1

Step 1 · Select the best point to land while the crew checks the main halyard will run free.

· Sail up tide of the landing area.

· Turn head to wind, drop the main and raise the centreboard.

Step 2 · Back the jib to turn the boat towards your chosen landing spot.

· As you approach the shore, lose speed by easing the jib sheet until the sail is flying free.

Step 3 · The crew jumps out and turns the boat into the wind as the helm raises or removes the rudder.

· If your boat has a forestay, drop the jib.

Step 2

Returning in waves requires co-ordinated help from a shore crew. Make sure you are aware of the system before sailing in and establish the signals to be used.

When the shore crew signal they are ready, begin your approach. To avoid surfing down a wave and burying the bow, follow the back of a wave in quickly, board raised and rudder released. Sail positively to the spot indicated and the shore crew will lift you and your boat clear before the arrival of the next wave.

Step 3

> **TOP TIP**
> To keep the halyard tangle free so the sail can be swiftly lowered, flake the coiled halyard over the windward side prior to un-cleating. It should trail behind the boat.

Picking Up a Mooring

The principles for picking up a mooring or coming alongside a boat or jetty are the same.

 Wind and Tide Together

- Run a mooring line from the bow in preparation.
- Sail to a position downwind of, and away from, the buoy.
- Approach on a close reach, controlling power and speed.
- Aim to bring the buoy onto the windward side of the bow. If the boat is moving too fast, sail away and try again.
- Once at the buoy, raise the centreboard as the crew secures the boat to the buoy, using a round turn and two half hitches or a bowline.
- Drop and stow the sails.

> GOLDEN RULE
>
> Make a steady and controlled approach, de-powering the boat fully so you lie to the tide.

When mooring a catamaran, attach a bridle line between both bows and the mooring, to prevent the boat from swinging or fouling the mooring chain.

> TOP TIP
>
> To determine the tidal flow, look at the mooring buoys. The small grab buoy will lie down tide of the large mooring buoy. A stronger current increases the distance between the two.

Wind and Tide Opposed

Position the boat upwind of the mooring buoy. Prepare to lower the mainsail.

Turn head to wind and lower the mainsail. Back the jib to turn the boat down wind and raise the centreboard.

Ease the jib to slow the boat as you make the final approach, helm controlling the jib as the crew prepares to take hold of the buoy.

Let the jib fly so the tide stops the boat at the buoy. The crew can now secure the boat.

In light winds and a strong tide, the jib might not have the power to carry you against the tide. In this situation, leave the mainsail up and approach from upwind. Lose speed by gradually lowering the main. Take care to sheet the main in a little to clear the shrouds.

Leaving a Mooring

If the boat is pointing into the wind, attach the rudder and hoist the sails whilst moored. Hoist the mainsail first to keep the boat pointing into the wind. Finally, hoist the jib, lower the board and slip the painter. Backing the jib will bring the bow away from the wind to put the boat on a reach. Sheet in and sail away. If wind and tide are opposed, attach the rudder and hoist the jib, leaving it to fly. Slip the mooring line and sail away under jib alone to a clear area. Prepare the mainsail; turn the boat into the wind and hoist before bearing away to continue sailing. It may be easier to turn head to wind if the mainsail is partially raised before leaving.

Coming Alongside a Fixed Object or Boat

Make your life easy by preparing first. Prepare mooring lines and deploy fenders if carried.

DVD **Wind and Tide Together**

- Approach your destination on a close reach.
- Control speed using the main sheet, letting the jib flap.
- Ease the sheets as you turn the boat gently alongside.
- Raise the board as the crew secures the boat.

DVD **Wind and Tide Opposed**

Lower the mainsail and make the same approach as a wind against tide mooring.

Wind Across Tide

With wind direction across the flow of the tide:

- With the landing area at right angles to the tide, approach slowly into the tide on a close reach. Turn into the wind to bring you to the down tide side of the landing (**A**).
- With the landing area parallel to the tide, approach on a close reach into the tide. If landing on the windward side, drop the mainsail and approach into the tide, under jib alone (**B**). If landing on the leeward side, ease sails fully to stop along side (**C**).

GOLDEN RULE
Although similar to mooring, there is a risk of collision; always plan an escape route.

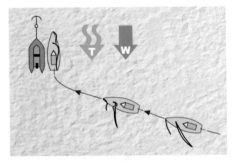
Caption

Caption

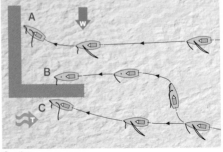
Caption

Anchoring

Many sailing dinghies and catamarans do not carry anchors, as the boats would not lie to an anchor in a stable position. However, keel boats and cruising dinghy sailors would consider an anchor absolutely essential. Tie the anchor down when not in use.

Select an appropriate anchorage. If necessary, use a chart and tide table to provide information regarding the nature of the seabed, obstructions, and the depth of water.

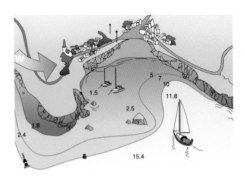

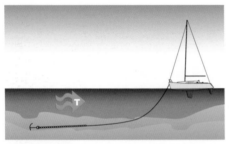

The length of chain ensures a more horizontal pull on the anchor

Before you start, prepare the anchor, ensuring it is attached to a strong point on the boat and will run freely from the bow. A short length of chain makes the anchor more effective. Line and chain should be at least three times the depth of water. The anchor line is known as a **warp**.

CQR general purpose anchor, good in sand and mud

Grapnel folds away very small

Approach: Wind and Tide Together

- Approach the chosen site on a close reach, using the main sheet to control the speed.

- Lower the jib if possible or let it fly. Release the main sheet to bring the boat to a stop.

- Lower the anchor over the windward side of the boat, and raise the centreboard. The mainsail will hold the boat's position relative to the wind as you drift back.

- Make sure the anchor is holding: check that two inline objects on the land do not change position in relation to each other, known as 'taking a transit'.

- When the anchor is holding, lower the mainsail.

- If the anchor is not holding, let out more warp. If this fails, retrieve the anchor and make another attempt.

TOP TIP

If you do not have a bow fairlead, run the anchor line through a small rope loop tied through a bow fitting. Looping around the forestay can snap it.

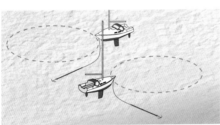

Consider how you will swing as the tide changes, will you be clear of hazards?

Leaving Your Anchorage

Leave using the same method as leaving a mooring, bringing the anchor on board rather than letting a mooring line go. Take care to bring it under the jib sheets to avoid tangles.

🄳🅅🄳 Heaving To

Heaving to is used whenever you wish to de-power the boat and hold it at a constant angle to the wind whilst floating free. This is a more stable position than simply lying to with both sails flapping, due to the jib being aback.

- Select a point with clear water downwind, or down tide, whichever is the stronger.

- Cleat the jib aback with the main sheet fully eased.

- Hold the tiller to leeward, and raise the centreboard half way.

- Maintain a good look out and be aware of leeway.

Approach: Wind and Tide Opposed

Anchor the boat into the tide, with the boat pointing downwind and the mainsail lowered.

Go head to wind upwind of your chosen spot and lower the mainsail.

Make the same approach as a wind against tide mooring.

When the boat is stopped in the correct place, lower the anchor and let the warp out as the boat drifts back in the tide.

Check the anchor is holding using a transit.

Taking a transit

GOLDEN RULE
Drop the anchor up-tide of where you want the boat to lie and allow room to swing if the tide turns.

15

Reefing Afloat In Strong Winds

As the wind becomes stronger, you may need to reduce sail area. Methods vary as different classes use a variety of reefing systems. Make life easy by reefing ashore, at a mooring or at anchor. If none of these are viable, sail into clear water and heave to.

Slab Reefing

A slab reefing system includes a rope fed from the boom through an eye in the leech of the sail. A second eye is situated at the luff, above the downhaul/Cunningham.

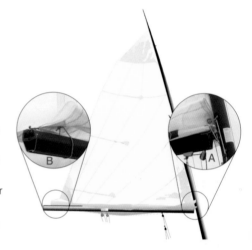

- To reef, partially lower the sail and feed the Cunningham through a higher eye in the luff. Pull tight (A).

- Pull the rope from the leech point to bring the eye down to the boom (B). With some systems you can do this first without lowering the sail.

- Many systems include elastic along the sail or boom to neatly hold the excess sail area.

- Many systems include a second or third rope and eyelets above the first to take further reefs.

Round the Boom
(Aft Mainsheet)

- Lower the sail about half way.

- Remove the kicking strap and mainsheet block from the boom and the lower batten from the sail.

- Tuck about 50cm of the leech down to the boom and roll with a reefing strop or sail bag to take the place of the kicking strap fixing point.

- Re-attach the main sheet and place the boom back on the goose neck.

- Hoist the sail, attach the kicking strap and sail away.

Putting a tuck in the mainsail leech

> TOP TIP
> Use a smaller jib with a reefed mainsail or reduce the jib using the roller mechanism.

Rolling a strop

Round the Mast

Most single-handed dinghies furl the sail around
the mast to reef or use a smaller mast and sail.
With the sail flapping, remove the kicker from
the mast and un-cleat the clew outhaul. Rotate
the base of the mast to furl the sail and then
simply re-attach the kicker and cleat the
outhaul.

Fully Battened Sails

When sailing in strong winds, de-power the sail
by pulling the Cunningham/downhaul on fully,
adding lots of kicking strap to bend the mast
and some outhaul to flatten the lower part of the
sail. The most common mistake is to sail with
too much power due to insufficient Cunningham
/ downhaul and kicker. Only a few fully
battened sails will reef, such as on the Dart 16.

A reefed catamaran sail is often flat and underpowered so be careful not to oversheet when sailing.

Ropework

Whipping the End of a Rope

Many modern ropes can be heat sealed at the
ends. If not, whipping twine can be used to
prevent fraying. (1) Lay a loop along the rope.
(2) Wind 10 – 20 turns over the loop very tightly.
(3) Finish by threading the end through the loop
(green arrow) and drawing it under the windings
with the yellow end.

Sheet Bend

This knot will join two lines of unequal thickness.

The double sheet bend is a more secure
version.

Fisherman's Bend

A good alternative to a bowline for attaching to a mooring buoy
or ring. The first half hitch is trapped under the round turn.

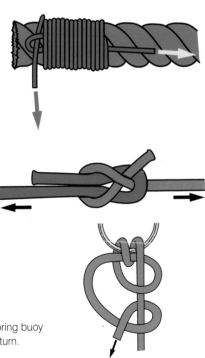

📀 Man Overboard (MOB)

Although it does not happen often, people can and do fall overboard when sailing. In some two-person dinghies, the boat may capsize after you lose someone over the side. With more stable boats you can sail back and recover your crew. Both the MOB and boat are equally influenced by the tidal flow so this does not need to be considered.

Step 1

Step 1 As soon as the crew falls overboard, regain control of the boat, check they are ok and signal your intention to return. Keep an eye on them at all times. Turn onto a reach, sailed correctly when the boom is held a few inches off the shrouds, and the sail still has some (not full) power.

Step 2 Leave the jib flapping and prepare to tack, allowing yourself plenty of room to slow the boat as you return. Tack and bear away onto a broad reach or reach.

Step 2

Step 3 Sail until you can approach on a close reach. If not furled, the flapping jib is a useful indicator.

Step 4 Once approaching on a close reach, de-power the main to control your boat speed. Stop with the MOB by the windward shroud. If the boat is still moving, twitch the tiller to windward to prevent the boat tacking on top of the MOB.

Step 3

Step 5 Bring the MOB aboard over the side or through the open transom, taking care not to bear away as you do so.

Step 4

> **TOP TIP**
> If uncertain about where to head up, point the boat toward the MOB. If the sail flaps to leeward you are in the right place. If still powered up, bear away and try again a little further on. If you find you are head to wind, sail past and tack round to try again on the opposite tack.

Step 5

Catamarans

Take great care not to capsize the cat after someone has fallen overboard. You may find yourself separated from your sailing partner and unable to right the boat. Many catamarans require two people to recover from a capsize. In addition, a capsized cat may blow downwind faster than you can swim.

After the MOB falls overboard, sail away on a reach.

Boats with Racks or Wings

If your boat has racks, most techniques remain the same. It is often easier to re-board the boat through the transom. Extra consideration is required when coming alongside. If coming alongside an inflatable safety boat, rest the rack on the tubes for stability.

Gybe around. This is a more reliable method of turning without proper jib control.

Recover the MOB over the forward beam between the two hulls. An exhausted MOB may find it easier to climb over the back beam.

TOP TIP
If your boat has racks and you are alongside an inflatable, ask the crew to sit on the rack and tube, locking the two boats together.

1 | Seamanship Skills

Sailing in Adverse Conditions

Sailing Without a Rudder

This exercise introduces important principles of boat control, and may be useful if you have a broken rudder. The boat is steered by altering the balance and sail setting. Practise in a clear area with a steady and light wind. This manoeuvre is not possible in catamarans.

- Sheet the mainsail in to luff up.
- Sheet the jib in to bear away.
- Heel to leeward to luff up.
- Heel to windward to bear away.

Before you start, raise the board by one third. Reef the mainsail if necessary.

Steer the boat using the following controls:

To avoid over-steering, practise by controlling jib and mainsail and balancing yourself. Learn to work with the crew later.

See **Performance Sailing** on page 76 for more information.

Sailing Without a Centreboard

If the centreboard is lost or damaged you will need to use another method to help the boat point to windward and minimise leeway. The easiest way is to move your weight to the bow, sinking the 'V' section down to act as an improvised board. The boat will not point as high and will make greater leeway, but some progress to windward is possible using this technique.

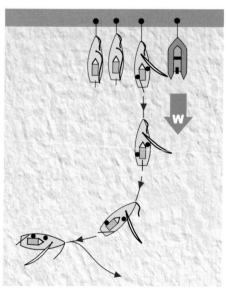

DVD **Sailing Backwards**

Sailing backwards can be really useful when leaving a crowded windward shore. Start with the boat stationary and directly head to wind, usually with the centreboard half down.

- Push the boom out against the shroud and back the mainsail. The sail will turn the stern away from the side it is set and drive the boat backwards.

- Counter the turn with a little rudder, tiller pushed away from the boom.

- Keep your weight towards the bow to lift the transom clear.

- To sail forwards, move the tiller towards the boom and sheet in main and jib. Straighten the tiller as the boat gathers way.

2 | Dealing with Inversion Capsizes

The best advice for dealing with inversions is try not to let it happen! If you do get to the stage where you know the boat is going to capsize, try to step over and onto the centre board to avoid the inversion altogether.

However, an inverted capsize should be a straightforward problem......provided the crew are aware of the risk of entanglement as the mast and rigging sinks. Most modern boats have self draining cockpits and will probably have no effective air pocket underneath once inverted. While likely to require bailing once uprighted, more traditional designs will probably retain an air void once inverted.

In the photograph above, the crew have moved to the stern in order to remain clear if the boat inverts. The crew is in a safe position to watch the helm onto the centreboard, where she can stabilise the boat on its side.

If the boat does invert both crew and helm move to the windward side and lean back on the centreboard, using a jib sheet to assist if necessary. Once the centreboard is within reach, the heavier person should climb onto it and bring the mast horizontal, pointing downwind.

Once the boat is stable in a horizontal position, the lighter person goes into the boat via the stern to drop the spinnaker and release kicker and mainsheet. Free the spinnaker halyard and carefully pull the downhaul to lower the spinnaker into the chute. If your boat has bags instead of a chute, gather the spinnaker using the upper sheet and then one side of the sail, stowing it in the upper bag.

GOLDEN RULE
Safety first. Stay in contact with the boat but take care if the boat is inverting.

Note that while this procedure will reduce the risk of the boat inverting on top of a crew member, some boats are more prone to inversion than others. Be aware of the risk of re-inversion at all times. One or two designs may even invert with someone fully on the centreboard.

Once the boat is ready, lean back to bring the boat up, scooping the crew aboard if possible

One very common problem is that the hull blows downwind of the rig. If the boat is righted from this position, the force on the sail is likely to capsize the boat on top of the unfortunate person who was on the centreboard. To avoid the problem, ask the crew to hang on to the toe straps to prevent the boat coming upright. Pull just the head of the sail out of the water so that the wind will spin it around to the leeward side. Then right the boat as normal. It is often easier to re-enter the boat over the stern. Once aboard grab the tiller, check the boat and prepare to sail off.

GOLDEN RULE
Always lower the spinnaker at least partially into the chute/bags before bringing the boat up. If you do not, you will almost certainly lose control of the righted boat or damage the spinnaker.

Multihull Capsizes

A full inversion can be solved by moving both crew and helm to the back of the leeward hull. The stern should sink, screwing the bows up. Use the righting line to pull the masthead to the surface.

Once the masthead is on the surface, move forward to the bows so that wind pressure on the trampoline will swing the mast into wind. This makes righting the boat easier as the wind lifts the sail.

3 | Day Sailing

Small boat cruising is a fascinating and relaxing pastime, whether your horizon is the far end of the reservoir or further afield. Cruising is as diverse in nature as the boats that are used. Sail Cruising is a very safe activity, providing you follow a few simple principles and plan your day to make the best use of the sailing area and conditions.

Equipment

Safety

The safety equipment you should carry will depend on the type of boat, the length and nature of the trip, and who is on board. Carry more rather than less, but not at the expense of weighing down the boat with things you are unlikely to use.

Catching cold and capsizing are the most common issues when sailing in the UK, so always wear a buoyancy aid or lifejacket and carry waterproofs.

If you are sailing in an area with few other boats, consider taking some means of communication in case of difficulty. Handheld VHFs or mobile phones are useful, but may fail to reach anyone depending on location. Boats sailing alone should always carry flares, which should be stored dry. Flares have a limited shelf life, so always replace them when the date has expired. Day/night flares are useful to signal your position when in sight of rescue, while parachute flares are more effective in attracting attention from a distance.

Pilotage

You will need to find your way around whilst afloat (pilotage). Small boat pilotage only requires simple equipment and will very much depend on location. It is easy to become disorientated even in moderate visibility so always carry a chart and compass on coastal trips. Do your planning in advance and keep it simple. Charts have a nasty habit of blowing away, so a waterproof notebook with a summary of the trip may be more practical, with a cut-out chart of the immediate area for backup.

3 | Day Sailing

Boat Choice, Setup and Stowing Gear

Choose a stable and sensible boat for cruising and certainly not one that capsizes easily. Many cruising sailors pay scant attention to rig tuning, but getting the mast position and rake right can make a huge difference to pointing ability – the difference between catching the tide and being several hours late. See **Performance Sailing** for more information.

Stow equipment low and central if possible

In theory, your equipment should be stowed low and central. Weight in the ends of a boat will make it handle clumsily. In practice, the crew normally occupies central space so a compromise is necessary. Class Associations can be an invaluable source of handy tips.

A small toolkit is useful for running repairs. This should include a collection of small spares such as shackles and split rings. A modern multi-tool can save space and weight.

An outboard engine and fuel may be worth carrying on some trips, but an anchor is always essential.

Weather Conditions

You do not need a detailed knowledge of weather in order to go small boat cruising. However, you do need to know what the weather will be doing during your trip. The key questions are: What wind and weather is coming? How will it affect conditions, such as the sea state? There are many different sources of weather forecast.

> **GOLDEN RULE**
> Always leave details of your route and expected time of return with a reliable person.

Radio	Radio 4 Shipping Forecast and local radio	Fax	Forecasts and synoptic charts
Coastguard	Marine safety information broadcast on VHF	Internet	Numerous sites including RYA website
Harbour Office	Posted outside daily	Email	Sent to you each weekend
Mobile Telephone	Text forecasts	Newspaper	General forecasts often with synoptic chart
Telephone	Recorded forecasts by area	Teletext	Ceefax, Oracle, etc

Predicting the Sailing Conditions

It pays to think about how local effects will combine with the general weather. Generally, there is more wind during the day, due to the heated air low down mixing with strong winds higher up. This is known as thermal mixing, and explains why the breeze usually abates around sunset as the temperature drops.

In general, if there are light **gradient winds** (the wind due to a high or low pressure system) in any direction and there is a difference in temperature between sea and land, there is likely to be a sea breeze.

On a sunny day in particular, the land heats up quickly, causing the air to rise. Replacement air is drawn in over the coastline - a sea breeze (fig. 1).

With a sea breeze in the same direction as the gradient wind, you may experience strong winds. Equally, if they are opposed and the gradient wind is strong, there may be a flat calm in the afternoon.

In general the sea breeze will tend to **veer** (rotate with the sun) through the day, often ending up parallel to the coastline by sunset.

The wind will tend to accelerate as it funnels past the projections or obstructions so an offshore breeze will tend to be turbulent and gusty (fig. 2).

Over land, the wind is slowed and backed (deflected in the opposite direction to the sun), so if the wind is blowing parallel to the coast, you may experience strong or lighter winds depending on its direction. As a rule of thumb, with the wind on your back and land on your left, the breeze will reduce as it diverges inland (A). With the wind on your back and land on your right, there will be convergence and the breeze will freshen (B). This effect can extend as far as a mile offshore.

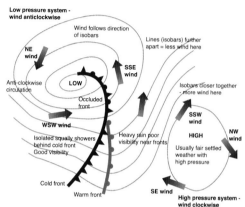

Low pressure system - wind anticlockwise

Wind follows direction of isobars

NE wind

Anti-clockwise circulation

LOW

Occluded front

WSW wind

Isolated squally showers behind cold front
Good visibility

Cold front

Warm front

SSE wind

Lines (isobars) further apart = less wind here

Isobars closer together - more wind here

SSW wind

Heavy rain poor visibility near fronts

HIGH

NW wind

Usually fair settled weather with high pressure

SE wind

High pressure system - wind clockwise

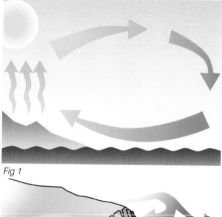

Fig 1

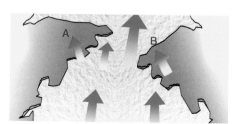

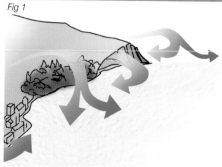

Fig 2

3 | Day Sailing

Tide induced wind

With no gradient wind, A and B are enjoying the sea breeze induced by a large island on a sunny day. A experiences less breeze as she moves in the tide. B is moved against the breeze and so feels more wind. Both boats will notice a difference when the tide turns.

Wind and tide will have a considerable impact on sea conditions. Wind and tide directly opposed (wind over tide) can produce big waves with breaking tops, particularly in the entrance to an estuary mouth or over a sandbar. It pays to ask locally what conditions are likely. Local knowledge is much better than theory.

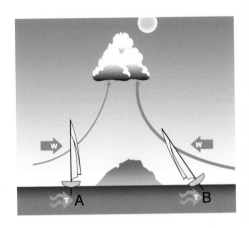

Passage Planning

Once you know a coastal area well, very simple planning and a weather forecast are often all that is required. In a less familiar or a complicated sailing area, it pays to plan in advance.

Interpreting Charts

Charts are a representation of the curved surface of the Earth on a flat sheet of paper. As a result charts are drawn using a system of latitude and longtitude as a grid reference and scale. Distance is always measured in degrees, minutes and seconds of latitude above the equator on a scale up the side of the chart. One minute of latitude is equal to one nautical mile (1 nautical mile = 1.12 statute miles). The vertical lines on the chart all relate to true north.

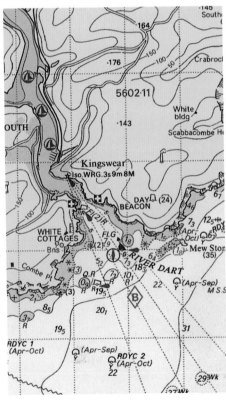

Like land maps, charts use symbols to show useful and important features and hazards. Here a birdseye view of Dartmouth shows how the chart relates to the coastline.

Symbols and Abbreviations (5011) published by the UK Hydrographic Office can be used to identify features and symbols on the chart.

 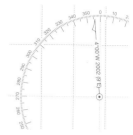

Depth of water shown is 'lowest astronomical tide' – the lowest tide likely to occur, known as Chart Datum.

The black line along the coast represents the highest water level normally occurring, i.e. the edge of the land.

Direction is indicated in degrees by the **compass rose** printed on the chart. The compass points to magnetic north, which changes a tiny amount each year - not significant for basic pilotage. The difference between north on the chart and magnetic north is known as **variation** and is marked on the chart's compass rose.

Pilotage in Practice

Course to steer

Although buoys mark channels, lining up two objects in transit is a very useful indication of a straight course.

If you are unable to see your objective, use a compass to steer your course. Compasses suffer from deviation, caused by ferrous or electrical objects in the boat, so your course may not be that accurate.

You should also allow for the tidal flow, and the aforementioned magnetic variation. On the compass rose above, the compass needle points to the west (or left) of the grid marked on the chart. This reduces the bearing so we must add 4 degrees to any course we work out on the chart.

Boat speed

Boat speed is measured in knots, or nautical miles per hour. 1 knot is therefore slightly more than 1 mile per hour. With practice you will be able to estimate your speed quite accurately.

Leeway

A small boat sailing to windward will slide sideways a little, particularly in waves. Estimate leeway by comparing your wake with the course steered. Allow about 5 degrees for leeway as a good starting point but you may need to allow considerably more.

Tidal Flow

Tidal streams around the UK are relatively strong and therefore are a major consideration when planning a trip. The level of the sea rises and falls as the tidal currents flow around the coast, resulting in two high tides and two low tides approximately every twenty five hours. Your trip can be speeded up, slowed, or the sea conditions altered by the tide.

The critical questions to ask when planning your trip are:

- When does the tide change direction?
- How much flow is there in which direction?
- Is there sufficient depth for a safe course?

Times and heights of high and low water can be found in a nautical almanac, but local tide tables available from yacht chandlers, sailing clubs or the harbour master's office provide all you need to know for local sailing. Remember to correct for BST by adding one hour if necessary.

The difference in height between each high water and the next low water is known as the **tidal range**. **Spring tides** occur at full and new moon, and have a bigger range and stronger flows than **neap tides**, which occur at half moons. In this example, the height of the evening tide varies between 0.7m and 4.8m above chart datum, a range of 4.1m.

Though the tide does not necessarily turn at high or low water, the approximate **height of tide** can be worked out using either the Rule of Twelfths or the Percentage Rule. For an example, see Appendix 1 (page 27).

For a more accurate picture of flow rates, refer to the nearest **tidal diamond** on the chart, together with it's associated table. Ensure you refer to the tide table for the correct standard port for your chart. Alternatively refer to a **tidal stream atlas**. Both diamonds and atlases show the hourly flow and direction for spring and neap tides, together with the direction of flow.

For a sample plan for a day sail, see Appendix 2 (page 40).

ENGLAND - DARTMOUTH

TIMES AND HEIGHTS OF HIGH AND LOW WATERS

13	0137	0.6
	0813	4.5
SA	1356	0.7
	2024	4.8

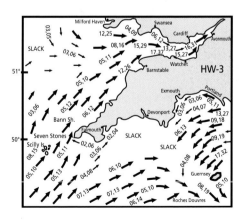

Pilotage with GPS (Global Positioning System)

A GPS receiver obtains a position fix from signals transmitted by orbiting satellites. The fix is generally accurate to within 15 metres and displayed on the GPS as latitude and longitude.

The simplest way to navigate with a GPS is to plot your latitude and longitude on a chart. A GPS set will give you much more information than this though, for example it will tell you your course and speed over the ground and your position relative to a **waypoint**.

Waypoints help you to navigate - they are positions on the chart that you can input and store in the memory of your GPS and use as reference points, such as the entrance of a harbour. When you activate a waypoint the GPS will display a lot of useful information that will help you fix your position and navigate to the waypoint.

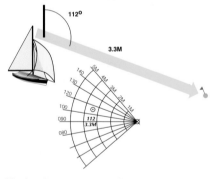

Navigating to a waypoint

The GPS will also tell you your **course over the ground (COG)** and **speed over the ground (SOG)**. Matching your COG to the bearing for a waypoint is a crude but useful way to stay on track. The GPS also uses your SOG to calculate your estimated time of arrival (ETA).

Fixing your position using a waypoint

The GPS displays the range (distance) and bearing to the waypoint. You can plot this directly on a chart using a plotter and pair of dividers.

A more convenient way of obtaining a fix is to pre-draw a 'web' of bearings and distances to your chosen waypoint on a chart. When on passage you can quickly compare the GPS display to the web. (**SOG**). Matching your COG to the bearing for a waypoint is a crude but useful way to stay on track. The GPS also uses your SOG to calculate your estimated time of arrival (ETA).

TOP TIP

GPS is generally reliable and accurate, but can go wrong. Always back up your position with another source of information. Keep a record of your position.

Buoyage

The IALA system of buoyage is used throughout
Europe. The system covers both lateral
buoyage (marking the sides of the channels)
and cardinal buoyage (marking hazards or
navigational features relative to compass
direction). The buoyage system is designed
principally for larger vessels.

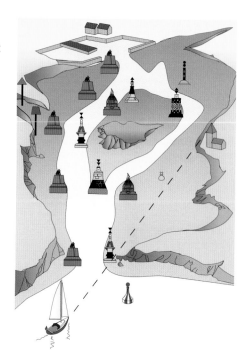

*Lateral port mark -
'red coke cans are
on the left'*

*North Cardinal -
'top points north'*

*Lateral starboard
mark*

Safe water

*West Cardinal -
'west is waisted'*

*South Cardinal -
'top points south'*

*East Cardinal -
'east is egg-shaped'*

*Isolated Danger -
'Dennis the Menace'*

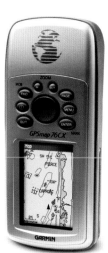

 🅳🆅🅳 Landing on a Shore

If you are cruising in a dinghy or shallow keelboat, you may well wish to go ashore at some point. Be aware that if land is privately owned there may be no right of access above the high water mark.

If the wind is at least slightly offshore you may be able to take the anchor up the beach, leaving the boat afloat. This will depend on any tidal stream. Plan for what will happen if the tide turns while you are ashore.

If you choose a lee shore, either sail ashore under jib only, or anchor close offshore and ease the boat back into shallow water to make your landing.

Again, beware of the tide; a change in the conditions may result in the boat swinging out of reach once you are ashore.

To depart, simply climb aboard, hoist sails and haul off using the anchor cable.

Decision Making During a Passage

Remember to leave details of your trip with a reliable person ashore and inform them of any change in plans. In this way you can be sure of the alarm being raised if you are late. If strong winds are forecast, or if you are caught out by too much/too little wind or bad weather, have an alternative plan ready and make decisions early. Remember that the sea state may change dramatically when the tide turns so keep a generous margin for error. Plan ahead, asking yourself how you would deal with different eventualities.

Passages in Strong Winds

When sailing in strong winds or waves, pay close attention to the 'five essentials': boat balance, trim, sail setting, centreboard and course made good.

- Reduce sail area or de-power the rig early rather than late – sailing at top speed may be thrilling but you can quickly become tired and make mistakes.

- Concentrate on balancing the boat and trim to stay dry – if your dinghy is punching into a heavy sea and water is coming into the boat, move back a little to lift the bow.

- Think carefully about where to sail for a sheltered passage or a more favourable tide.

- Look out for confused water, indicating strong tides or shallow water.

- Keep an eye out for other boats.

- Above all, make safe, seamanlike and conservative decisions.

Appendix 1

Estimating the Height of Tide (H.O.T.)

The height of tide at any time can be estimated reasonably accurately using one of two rules. The idea is to estimate the amount that the tide has accumulated or fallen in each hour. The flow accelerates and decelerates so the amount of water accumulated each hour is different. Note that you should still leave a margin for error.

This example refers to Dartmouth on 13th July as on page 23 of Day Sailing

From the tide table, the range after the morning high water is 4.5 - 0.7 = 3.8m

For the Percentage Rule:

10% of range = 10% of 3.8 = 0.38m, say 0.4m.

For the Rule of Twelfths:

1/12 of range = 1/12 of 3.8 = 0.32m, say 0.3m

Time	Percentage Rule Percentage subtracted	Twelfths Rule Twelfths subtracted	H.O.T. above chart datum (m) %	Twelfths
HW	-	-	4.5	4.5
HW+1	10%	1/12	4.1	4.2
HW+2	15%	2/12	3.5	3.6
HW+3	25%	3/12	2.5	2.7
HW+4	25%	3/12	1.5	1.8
HW+5	15%	2/12	0.9	1.2
LW	10%	1/12	0.5	0.9

To obtain an approximate depth at any time, add the **height of tide** (**H.O.T.**) to the depth indicated on the chart at that point.

So, for example, 2 hours after high water, the depth at any charted point can be estimated by taking the H.O.T. at high water and subtracting the amount of water which has flowed away. This will be 25% or 3/12 of the range.

So where 7.9 m is indicated on the chart, depth at HW+2 = 7.9 + 3.5 = 11.4m using Percentage Rule.

Appendix 2

Sample Plan for a Day Sail from Dartmouth

Step 1: Decide on your trip and obtain tidal and weather information

Tom wants to explore the estuary in his keelboat starting from Kingswear but also to sail along the coast to Brixham, a distance of 5 miles. Local high water at Dartmouth is around 9 am, but Tom will need to look at the high water times for Plymouth because the tidal diamonds on the chart are referred to that port.

The weather forecast is S Force 2 becoming S Force 3. It is bright and sunny; local knowledge suggests that the sea breeze will increase this to Force 4 veering to the SW in the late afternoon.

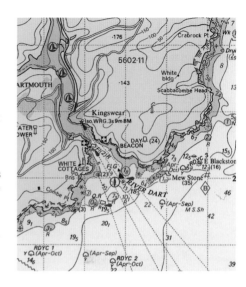

The nearest high water to his proposed departure time on 13th July is 0851 BST, say 0900 BST. The most appropriate diamond to use is ⑧ as it is located in the area of his passage.

The tidal flows listed for tidal diamond B shows that the tidal flow will carry him north-east along the coast until some time between 1300 and 1400, when the flow reverses. (Tom could also have obtained the same information from a Tidal Stream Atlas.)

Step 2: Predict the conditions you will experience

Tom is confident sailing in the estuary but concerned about the coastal passage. Wind and tide are together until the tide turns so he expects a fairly calm sea. Visibility will be moderate so he carries a radio as well as flares.

Step 3: Predict how long each part of the passage will take

This will be a combination of the boat's speed and direction with the tidal flow and direction.

On the outward journey Tom's boat can sail

(boat speed) at up to 6 knots downwind. He expects to manage only 3 - 4 knots in the conditions.

If he explores Dartmouth harbour until 1130 and then departs, there will be a favourable tide of 0.5 knots for the first hour, reducing to 0.1 knots before the tide turns between 1300 and 1400.

ENGLAND - PLYMOUTH
TIMES AND HEIGHTS OF HIGH AND LOW WATERS

13 0138 0.8
　　　 0751 5.1
SA 1357 0.9
　　　 2002 5.4

PA 38:
Tidal Streams referred to HW at PLYMOUTH

Hours		Geographical Position	A 50°13'0N 3 37·1W		B 50°17'0N 3 35·1W		
		Directions of streams (degrees)	Rates at spring tides (knots)	Rates at neap tides (knots)			
Before High Water 6		203	2·2	1·1	206	1·0	0·5
5		203	2·1	1·1	208	1·2	0·6
4		192	1·5	0·8	213	1·0	0·5
3		137	0·7	0·4	235	0·5	0·3
2		057	2·9	1·4	072	0·3	0·2
1		043	3·0	1·5	044	0·7	0·3
High Water		046	2·5	1·2	039	1·2	0·6
After High Water 1		049	2·2	1·1	031	1·1	0·5
2		061	1·4	0·7	035	0·8	0·4
3		137	0·7	0·4	044	0·5	0·2
4		186	1·5	0·8	046	0·1	0·1
5		200	2·1	1·0	214	0·5	0·2
6		202	2·2	1·1	209	0·8	0·4

Combining the tidal flow with the boat speed suggests a speed over the ground of:

1130 to 1230 boat speed + tide = 3 + 0.5 = 3.5 nautical miles
1230 to 1330 boat speed + tide = 3 + 0.1 = 3.1 nautical miles

1130 to 1330 total distance covered = 3.5 + 3.1 = 6.6 nautical miles.

Tom should therefore reach Brixham comfortably about the same time as the tide turns against him.

He can explore the harbour on a rising tide before his departure for Brixham, provided there is enough breeze to carry him over the tide in the harbour, where flows will be stronger, and enough water to sail. He can check the height of tide (H.O.T.) using the method shown in **Appendix 1**.

Having stopped for food and explored a little, Tom reckons he might set off at 1530. The tidal diamond shows a tidal stream of between 1.0 and 0.5 knots towards Dartmouth until1730. Unfortunately the wind may by then be veering to the SW. Sea conditions will therefore be quite choppy making it a wetter journey than the outward trip.

In the fresher breeze, Tom decides to reef, estimating that his boat speed will still be about 3 knots. He will be tacking, reducing his **speed over the ground (S.O.G.)** to perhaps 2 knots.

1530 to 1630 boat speed plus tide = 2 + 1.2 = 3.2 knots
1630 to 1730 boat speed plus tide = 2 + 1.0 = 3.0 knots

Achieving 6.2 nautical miles before 1730 ensures that he should cover the 5 nautical miles comfortably before the tide turns again at that time.

When does the tide turn?
The tidal diamond information refers to 30 minutes each side of the indicated time:

Published Data:			**Means:**		
1200	044	0.5	1130 - 1230	044°	0.5 knots
1300	046	0.1	1230 - 1330	046°	0.1 knots
1400	214	0.5	1330 - 1430	214°	0.5 knots

So, in this example, the tide turns from NE to SW at 1330. There will, of course, be a period of slack water but the tidal diamonds sometimes do not show this clearly.

Step 4: Alternatives
The outward journey should be predictable. However, the strength and direction of the afternoon sea breeze will be difficult to predict exactly. If conditions are too rough on the return journey, Tom plans to simply turn around early and broad reach back to Brixham against the tide, where he will be stuck overnight.

Though no overfalls (rough seas) are shown on the chart, it would be wise to approach Berry Head with caution in case there are strong tidal eddies close inshore.

On the other hand, if the sea breeze does not materialise due to cloudy weather, Tom may find the breeze remains southerly and have an easy return trip with the tide behind him.

4 | Sailing with Spinnakers

Over the years, dinghy and catamaran sailing has undergone a number of far reaching changes...

In the Thirties, Uffa Fox introduced planing dinghies. In the Sixties, the ability to plane to windward was developed. In the Eighties, Julian Bethwaithe developed the asymmetric spinnaker and completed the logical gybing downwind technique. Many of these developments have evolved through lighter equipment and better materials, some through better techniques.

As dinghies have got faster, theory and practice for dinghies, catamarans and windsurfers have merged. High performance dinghy sailing now takes place in **apparent wind**, just as it does for high performance cats and planing windsurfers.

This chapter looks at the impact of apparent wind whilst planing downwind and the difference between **conventional** and **asymmetric spinnakers**.

DVD Steering

As soon as the maximum righting force is exerted on a boat, by hiking or trapezing, steering controls the balance of the boat. With a spinnaker flying, modern rigs develop tremendous power. To control excess power (sailing in the Power Zone), bear away and reduce the heeling moment (balance) on the boat. To steer positively, keep the tiller extension as close as possible to a right angle with the tiller. Consider where you are sitting in the boat and change your steering style to suit, either pan handle or dagger grip.

TOP TIP
The lighter and faster the dinghy the more the relevance of apparent wind.

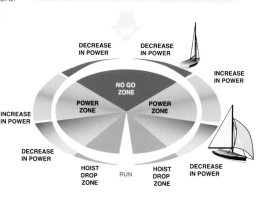

GOLDEN RULE
Steering controls power when sailing downwind. Bear away in gusts and luff up in the lulls to keep the boat level.

Helming dagger grip style

The helm has moved forward and changed to pan handle grip

Conventional and Asymmetric Spinnakers

The conventional spinnaker was developed to gain better speed downwind. With the heeling forces greatly reduced downwind, it was possible to fly this specialist sail while running and gain considerable speed without excessive heeling. Originally only flown on runs, sailors soon developed the skill of sailing slightly higher to gain speed.

As sailors in the development classes were at the forefront of these changes it was no surprise to see more specialist sails being created by the Australian 18 foot class. Races were won by gybing conventional spinnakers downwind and sailing much greater distances at a significant speed advantage in these planing hulls.

Eventually, this led to the creation of an asymmetric spinnaker, which was not only better suited to sailing higher angles but also simplified the spinnaker systems.

Instead of controlling the height and angle of the conventional pole, the entire technique was changed to hoisting, gybing and dropping the spinnaker from a fixed pole. Because the gybing pole was replaced with a single, central pole, gybing had become as easy as swopping the jib from starboard to port or vice versa.

As a result of these developments, there is a clear choice in the performance boat market between boats with different types of spinnaker, each with its own strengths and disadvantages.

> TOP TIP
> If you can fly a conventional spinnaker you will find moving to an asymmetric easier than from an asymmetric to a conventional.

Stowage

The spinnaker (conventional or asymmetric) is stowed in either a bag or a chute. The chute option is the easiest to control as the spinnaker can be retrieved back into the boat by pulling on the downhaul line and storing the spinnaker in the chute sock.

Conventional spinnaker layout

Rigging Tips

Tie the spinnaker sheets together to stop ends tangling and allow better control when gybing. On asymmetric spinnakers, make sure that the attachment to the sail is as small as possible so it can be pulled around the front of the jib.

Larks foot the sheet to an asymmetric spinnaker

Asymmetric spinnaker layout

1 Spinnaker 2 Spinnaker pole
3 Stowage chute / sock 4 Spinnaker sheets tied together 5 Downhaul / retrieval line
6 Jib car on track 7 Storage bag

TOP TIP

Always check your spinnaker before going afloat. Asymmetric check: start at the tack, run up the luff to the head, then down the leech to the clew. Check that the spinnaker sheets go round the jib and are over the retrieval line.

Asymmetric Spinnaker Handling

Once hoisted, the sail develops a lot of power, so steering is the key. The steering must balance the forces on the boat. The crew cannot move into the boat until the sideways force on the boat is decreased by steering the boat away from the wind (see Power Zone diagram on page 30). To hoist, gybe or drop, bear away into the hoist/drop zone to decrease the power on the boat. The exact angle needed will be wind and boat dependent. The stronger the wind and the faster the boat, the lower we sail. Very fast boats in a Force 5 will almost be running in order to decrease the load and allow the crew to go into the boat to hoist the spinnaker. When turning from a beat to a broad reach you will go through an area (at about beam reach) where the forces will increase (**Step 1**). In strong winds, turn through this zone as quickly as possible (**Step 2**).

Once on a broad reach/run and in the hoist / drop zone the crew can hoist the spinnaker (**Step 3**). Depending on the boat this may be one halyard that pulls out the pole as well as hoist the spinnaker, or two. Hoist as quickly as possible or the spinnaker may catch in a wave at the front of the boat (**Step 4**). If it does catch, quickly hoist the spinnaker up out of the water before the boat slows down.

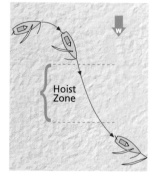

Once the spinnaker is hoisted (**Step 5**) the helm turns the boat higher into the wind, enters the Power Zone and exposes the spinnaker (which has until now been blanketed by the mainsail). At the same time, the crew sheets in the sail until it fills. Now ease the sail until the luff starts to curl (see **Trimming** overleaf).

As the boat accelerates, the crew and helm both hike or trapeze to balance the forces on the boat. The higher you sail (steering) the more balance is needed to offset the heeling forces. The spinnaker and mainsail must be trimmed correctly, otherwise the boat will not accelerate and the forces on the boat will quickly build and generate large amounts of heel with lower speed.

If the spinnaker has an 'hourglass' twist after hoisting, try gybing to free it.

Step 1

Step 2

Step 3

Step 4

Step 5

Trimming

Trimming asymmetric spinnakers could not be easier. Just concentrate on the luff of the sail. Ease the sheet until the sail starts to roll over (approx 6") and then gently roll it back.

Ease the spinnaker until the luff rolls *Oversheeted choking the air flow* *Correctly sheeted at full power*

By repeating this procedure constantly on the downwind leg the spinnaker will always be trimmed at the optimum angle to the wind.

🔵DVD Steering and balance

With the crew constantly looking at and trimming the spinnaker, the helm controls the balance by steering. If you are overpowered and start to heel, simply bear away. Likewise, if you are in a lull you can increase power by steering higher. Each different design of dinghy will have an optimum angle for the conditions and this is where experience of a particular design pays. To gain this knowledge, experiment against similar boats or attend class association training weekends.

The skill is to spot the gust and anticipate the extra sideways force as it lands, bearing away as the boat accelerates. Note that with large spinnakers, the effect of moving body weight further out will be minimal.

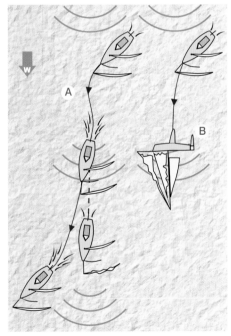

> **TOP TIP**
> When racing fast boats you may have to sail higher and further to induce planing. You should make a gain over other boats not planing as the apparent wind builds and heads.

A spots the approaching gust

A bears away as the gust lands and accelerates. **B** fails to adjust and capsizes

As the gust passes, **A** should luff again to maintain speed

(DVD) Gybing the Spinnaker

The speed with which you steer through the gybe must reflect the ability of the crew members to move across the boat. If you turn the boat too fast the forces on the boat will create excessive heeling. Communication between helm and crew is vital as you move in a co-ordinated manoeuvre. Plan the manoeuvre together beforehand.

Helm
Concentrate on steering. Greater speed into the gybe reduces the load on the rig, making gybing easier. As it gets windier, you will need a correction factor in the turn to send the boat back down onto a broad reach/run - the 'M' gybe. Judge this by mainsheet loads and help the boom across with your mainsheet hand. Let the mainsheet run out to allow the boom to go all the way to the shroud in higher winds (use a knot in the mainsheet to control this).

Crew
Prepare the new sheet before the gybe by taking up the slack. As you ease your weight inboard in preparation for the gybe, keep setting the spinnaker (normally by easing the sheet). When the helm calls "Gybe-Ho", start to move across the boat and pull on the old sheet to flatten the spinnaker across the jib. As you move to the new side of the boat, pull on the new sheet and allow the old one to run free. As the spinnaker inflates on the new gybe ease it until it is set with a small curl in the luff. Sit out harder or trapeze to set the course and balance.

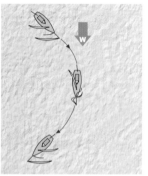

Steer a gentle curve to gybe in normal conditions

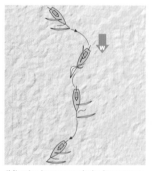

'M' gybe in strong winds: bear away, gybe, then bear away again to balance before adjusting course

TOP TIP
Aim to turn the boat so that both helm and crew can sit on the new windward side deck. The stronger the wind, the smaller the angle you will turn through to gybe.

📀 Dropping the Spinnaker

As many spinnaker chute systems will be rigged on the port side of the boat, dropping on port will involve pulling the spinnaker around the jib. It's better to drop on starboard if possible. If you have to drop on port, bear away onto a run which will take the sideways wind pressure off the spinnaker and allow an easier drop. A good indicator is if the luff of the sail has moved to windward of the bow.

Step 1

Step 1 Bear away to allow the crew to go into the boat. To control the spinnaker, the crew stands on the sheet or passes it to the helm. Take up the slack in the retrieval line and un-cleat the halyard. If there is a separate pole outhaul, uncleat this too.

Step 2 Pull as quickly as possible to prevent the spinnaker going in the water. The helm will need to steer carefully to keep the boat balanced: the trick is to steer to keep the hull directly under the mast.

Step 3 On some boats, complete the drop by transferring from the retrieval line to the sail to pull it fully into the boat. Tidy up the sheets and re-cleat the halyard.

Step 2

Step 3

TOP TIP

Continuous rolling can be a problem downwind. On asymmetrics check the centreboard is down. Crew and helm sit still and helm steers to counteract the roll.

📀 **Symmetrical Spinnaker Handling**

The symmetrical spinnaker is a little more complex to fly. This section primarily addresses launching from bags as launching from a chute is easier and is treated as if it is a leeward launch from a bag.

Leeward Hoist/Chute Hoist

Step 1 Attach the pole to the guy and the uphaul/downhaul rope to the pole. Then attach the pole to the mast. The pole should hook onto the mast with the hook facing up, for easy retrieval.

Step 2 Bear away so that the spinnaker can be hoisted. One crew member hoists while the other attends to sheet and guy.

Step 3 If you are on a broad reach or a reach, put the guy in a reaching hook or pull it down using a twinning line. This allows you to hike or trapeze and cuts down the stretch in the guy.

Step 4 Once fully up, pull on the guy until the pole touches the clew of the spinnaker. Now pull back until the pole and clew of the spinnaker are at approximately right angles to the wind. The pole height should allow the two clews to fly at the same height.

TOP TIP

To check pole height, ease the spinnaker sheet. The luff should fold in the middle and peel towards the head and foot. Peeling from the top or bottom indicates the pole is at the wrong height.

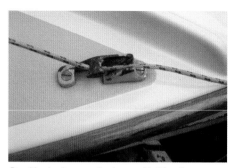

Reaching hooks are a simple way of holding the guy down and cleating it

Twinning lines provide greater control

(DVD) Windward Hoist

Depending on the previous drop, the spinnaker may be in the windward bag. Throw the spinnaker around the forestay and jib before putting up the spinnaker pole. **Step 1** Gather the spinnaker in your hands and upon a call from the crew/helm, throw it forward and in front of the forestay. At the same time the helm hoists as quickly as possible. **Step 2** The wind will blow the spinnaker to the new side. **Step 3** Now attach the spinnaker pole as before and set the guy at the correct angle.

Step 1   *Step 2*   Step 3

Trimming the Spinnaker

Trimming symmetric spinnakers is very similar to asymmetrics, except that the pole angle must be correct as on page 37. Sheet in until the luff of the sail is just curling. If the curl starts at the top or the bottom, re-adjust the pole height using the uphaul / downhaul.

TOP TIP
Throw the spinnaker sharply forwards around the forestay rather than upwards.

Gybing the Spinnaker

The sequence for gybing will vary depending upon what type of twinning line/ reaching hook you use. Hold down the twinning lines before the gybe to depower the spinnaker and give greater control. Release the lines after the gybe. (Alternatively, the helm can choke the kite behind the mainsail by holding both the sheet and guy).

There are numerous ways to gybe conventional spinnakers. The key is to have a system and stick to it, while playing to your strengths. If the helm is good at steering he may steer with the tiller between his legs and trim the guy and sheet during the gybe. Alternatively the guy and sheet may be cleated off for the gybe. Whatever system you use, commitment and speed is vital.

Run-to-run gybe

As with asymmetric spinnaker manoeuvres, steering is the key. Aim to follow the spinnaker round, while balancing the forces acting on the boat.

Step 1 The crew rotates the spinnaker back towards the wind by pulling on the guy, whilst the helm initiates the gybe with a small amount of rudder movement. **Step 2** The boom is helped across the boat as the spinnaker pole is transferred from the mast to the new guy. At this point, the pole may be on both new guy and old guy. Take the pole from the old guy and attach it to the mast.
Step 3 Place the new guy in the reaching hook / twinning line and carry on trimming as before.

Step 1

Step 2

Step 3

Gybing run-to-run is easier than reach-to-reach because the boat turns through a smaller angle. During a reach-to-reach gybe, pull the spinnaker much further round the forestay. In this type of gybe the sail may well collapse.

TOP TIP
If you struggle to remove the pole from the mast ease the downhaul line a little before the gybe.

📀 Dropping the Spinnaker into Bags

The spinnaker is best dropped on the windward side. If you are racing using bags, consider which gybe to drop from, in order to facilitate a leeward hoist at the next windward mark. Remove the pole from the mast; fly the kite until the correct distance from the mark. Store the pole and drop the spinnaker halyard, while pulling the leech down and into the windward bag. The foot will lie on the foredeck, until the entire spinnaker is in the bag.

For a chute drop, simply pull the spinnaker into the chute with the downhaul and then store the pole.

TOP TIP

Working down one leech stops twists. Never put the two clews together to gather in as this creates twists.

Apparent Wind

Apparent wind is the sailing domain of lightweight planing dinghies, catamarans and windsurfers. It is the combination of true wind (the wind you feel while stopped) and the wind created by your own speed. Remarkably, it has two significant advantages:

It is shifted further forward than the true wind.

It is stronger than the true wind.

When you bear away to handle stronger winds (2), you will have to bear away still further to allow for the apparent wind being forward (3). This double advantage enables very deep angles to be sailed on a windward/leeward course.

This is a relatively simplistic approach and you will need more detail as you gain experience.

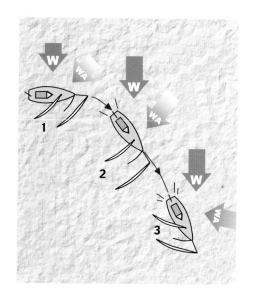

Dinghies and Skiffs

Displacement dinghies and **skiffs** are at opposite ends of a continuum. At one end, we have dinghies that will only plane in very strong winds. At the other, we have skiffs which plane upwind and downwind in light breezes.

The skiff is characterised by very light weight and significant righting ability via wings, trapeze or both. The skiff also has a very flat **rocker** that aids planing but hinders light wind performance. In general, the skiff is better suited to the advanced sailor as it places a significant emphasis on technique. However, most skiff types have large rudder blades for easier control. Because they sail fast downwind, pressure on the rig is low and gybing is relatively easy.

TOP TIP

Losing control? Bear away into the safe zone to regain balance and reduce power.

5 | High Performance Safety

Modern dinghies are easy to sail very fast. Think ahead, leave plenty of room for manoeuvres and keep a good lookout, particularly under spinnaker.

If you do capsize, be aware of the risk of entanglement in standing or running rigging or even the tiller extension. Trapeze hooks do occasionally foul on parts of the rigging, which can lead to an alarming or dangerous incident. To reduce the risk:

- Keep rope lengths to a minimum to avoid tangles

- Re-tension or replace tensioning elastic regularly. Slack wire or string is a hazard

- Carry a really sharp knife with a serrated edge

- Sail under control, not out of control

- Always tidy up loose sheet falls

A sharp knife is essential for safety

One of the worst things that can happen is for the crew to become entangled as the boat inverts. It is much better to avoid this problem than to solve it. Consider how you would deal with entanglements on your particular boat.

Know your boat. Under what circumstances will it invert? How quickly? Is there an air gap?

If this boat inverts now, the crew will be at risk

6 | Trapezing

In order to exert the maximum righting leverage, many boats are provided with racks, a trapeze wire, or both, to enable the crew to move further out. Trapezing is generally less tiring and more fun than hiking. Most trapeze boats are equipped with spinnakers. There are a few exceptions including some multihulls.

Trapeze Harnesses

A good harness should fit snugly and offer minimal opportunities for snagging on rigging etc. The hook should be positioned near your centre of gravity, and hooks into a ring suspended from the trapeze wire. The ring will be of adjustable height, so that you can raise and lower yourself according to the amount of leverage required and whether you are positioned forward or back. Good non-slip footwear is essential.

 Getting Out

The trapeze wire will always tend to pull you forwards, so lead with your front foot. In general, the front leg supports your weight and the back leg is used for balance, if necessary to lean towards the back of the boat a little.

Step 2 *Step 3*

Step 1 Grab the handle with your front hand and hook on with your back hand

Step 2 Take your weight on the trapeze wire and move out onto the side of the boat or rack, taking the jib or spinnaker sheet with you. Use your back hand for support if necessary but keep your weight on the trapeze ring, not your hands.

Step 3 Step out of the boat with your front foot. Take care not to over sheet as you move out.

Step 4 Follow with the back foot and relax your shoulders into the harness. You can then release the handle. While initially you may find the sheet useful to keep your balance, try to be aware of your balance through your feet.

TOP TIP - Start with the trapeze ring high, an easier position. Lower yourself as you gain confidence.

Step 4

6 | Trapezing

🔘DVD On the Trapeze

Traditionally, the crew trapezes flat for maximum leverage. However modern asymmetric boats have low freeboard, so a higher position is increasingly common. With your body at an angle it is easier to move in and out, you are clear of waves and have better all round visibility.

Teamwork is important and in gusty conditions the helm may move inboard to enable the crew to stay out. Equally, the crew may hold the helm's shoulder for stability in certain conditions. Sailing downwind you may need to move well back and lower yourself on the wire.

The classic trapeze position: feet close together but body straight and just clear of waves

A gust has landed. The helm has born away, the crew and helm have moved back to keep the bow up

Getting In

To come off the trapeze, reverse the procedure for getting out. Bend the front leg, holding the sheet in your rear hand and using this hand for support. While in traditional boats you may unhook from the ring in a sitting position, most asymmetrics require that you stay on your feet as you tack or gybe the boat.

Capsizing from the Trapeze

If you capsize to leeward, try to lower yourself into the water, unhooking from the trapeze ring first. If you jump you may damage sails or rigging, or worse, become entangled yourself. If you are quick you may manage to climb directly onto the centreboard.

A windward capsize will be very wet. Your priority once capsized will be to unhook yourself quickly and move to the back of the boat, clear of the sails etc., as the boat settles on its side.

TOP TIP - Communication is crucial with the crew on the trapeze. Warn the crew before altering course and discuss how to share responsibilities e.g. under spinnaker, crew concentrates on trimming spinnaker and helm watches for gusts and traffic.

7 | Start Racing

There are hundreds of sailing clubs throughout the UK. They nearly all organise regular racing along with training and social events.

Racing is normally at weekends, with some clubs carrying on through the winter months. During the summer, most clubs also sail on some weekday evenings.

Clubs provide storage space for dinghies and a regular meeting place for people with an interest in sailing.

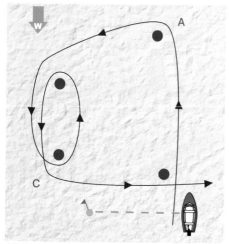 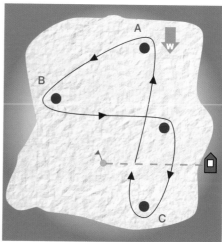

A is the windward mark, B is an offwind mark, C is the leeward mark

If there are sufficient boats of the same class, it is normal to organize a separate start. However it is possible to run races together with many different types of dinghy using a handicap system called the RYA Portsmouth Yardstick Scheme. Portsmouth Yardstick Scheme

The RYA Portsmouth Yardstick Scheme

The RYA Portsmouth Yardstick Scheme is a method of applying handicaps to sailing boats to allow different types of boat to compete on level terms.

It is based on the race results sent in by sailing clubs at the end of each year. From these the Portsmouth Numbers can be worked out or updated. Essentially each type of boat is allocated a Portsmouth Number (PN) roughly based around a thousand, the lower the number the faster the boat. If a boat with a PN of 950 takes 950 seconds to go around a course, a boat with a number of 1050 should cover the same course in 1050 seconds.

Starting a Race

A race is started with a countdown leading to all the boats crossing a line usually from the downwind side and going towards a buoy somewhere upwind. The start line is as sighted between two points, either buoys, masts on boats, or markers on the land.

The aims of a good start are as follows:

- To cross the start line immediately after the start signal
- To be traveling at full speed as soon as possible
- To be able go upwind by the best route, unhindered by other boats

- To not have other boats close enough to you to slow you down
- To cross the start line at the most advantageous point

20 seconds to go. A and B in clear air

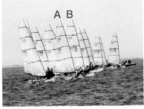

5 seconds to go. Accelerating to the line

5 seconds after the start. A and B are clear ahead at full speed

Explanation of signals

Unlike in athletics, a premature starter does not necessarily result in a restarted race. Instead, the race officer will sound another signal and raise the 'X' flag. This informs the sailors that somebody jumped the start and they must turn around and re-cross the line.

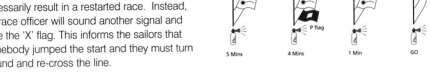

Individual Recall X

General Recall

Postponement

Preparatory P

Disqualification

1 Minute Rule

However, if several boats start early the race officer will start the race again. He can, on subsequent starts, use different flags in place of the 'P' flag to signal different penalties to deter people from starting early.

For more information refer to the rules book and your club sailing instructions

TOP TIP - The sound signals are use to draw sailors attention to the visual signals (the flags). Take your timing from the visual signals.

Where on the starting line?
Aim to start in clean air - as clear of other boats as possible.

One of the most important rules in sailing is the port/starboard rule. A boat on port tack must keep clear of a boat on starboard tack. Because the start inevitably has lots of boats going up wind, close to each other, it is generally easier to start on starboard tack.

A windward boat must keep clear of a leeward boat, **B** and **C** must keep clear of **A** on the line.

Square line
If the starting line is exactly at right angles to the wind, there is no advantage in starting at one end or the other. The distance to the windward mark will be the same and **A**, **B** and **C** start equally.

Bias
If the start line is not quite at right angles to the wind then one end of the starting line will be further upwind than the other and therefore nearer to the first buoy. The line is said to be biased. Sail along the line in both directions, with your mainsail right out. The end you can sail away from more easily is the one to start from. A leads B.

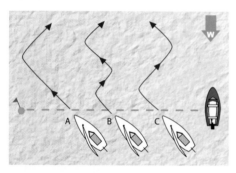

Room to accelerate
Get the boat going as fast as you can, as quickly as you can. It takes several seconds to accelerate a boat to full speed when going to windward. Sail faster as you approach the line by aiming 10 degrees or so off the wind, provided that you have room to leeward. **A** starts fastest.

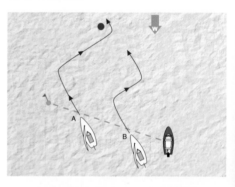

How do I know when I'm on the line?
It is very difficult to judge whether or not you are on the imaginary line, so it is worth taking a transit. Sail beyond the start line, sight along it and find an object on shore that is on the line. You can now tell if you are up to the start line (or not) by sighting the end of the line with the object beyond it. Be aware that quite a lot of the boat protrudes in front of you. A reads the transits and starts on time.

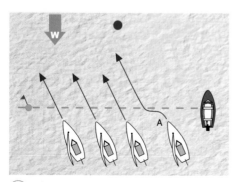

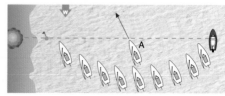

Going Up The Beat

Making best use of the breeze

Because the wind rarely comes from a consistent direction for very long, big advantages can be achieved by being on the tack that takes you nearest to the windward mark. Changes in wind direction tend to occur during gusts and lulls and keen eyed sailors will see their effect on the water before they arrive. With good communication between the helm and crew you can be ready to tack if the wind **heads** you (takes you further away from the windward buoy) or turn upwind a little if the wind **lifts** you (takes you nearer the windward buoy). **A** notices the header and tacks, then tacks again when the wind oscillates back. **A** is ahead of **B**.

The boat should be sailed as fast as possible (see Performance Sailing). Generally, the boat should be level (balanced) with the sails in tight and the controls adjusted to suit the wind strength.

Which side of the beat?

You can make gains upwind by traveling up the most advantageous side of the beat. As you tack going up the beat you travel to the left and the right hand side of a straight line to the windward buoy. Very often the wind or the water flow on one side will be more advantageous than on the other.

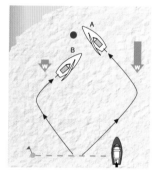

A Sails in more wind than B. A leads

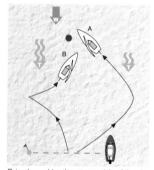

B is slowed by the strong tide. A leads

Tacking for the mark

A lay line is the imaginary line that extends down from the windward buoy depicting a windward course to the buoy. Tack to get to the windward buoy as soon as possible. C tacks late and falls behind A and B.

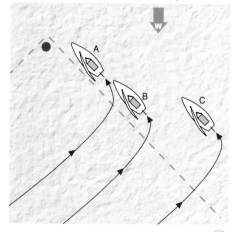

TOP TIP - Extra effort in the first 60 seconds after the start can put you in clean air and allow you to tack without other boats in the way.

At the Windward Mark

Tactics

- Approach on starboard tack if possible, to gain right of way over boats on port tack.
- Locate the next buoy before you get to the windward buoy, so you are ready to turn straight on to the new course.
- Ease the kicking strap before, and raise the centreboard after, you turn.
- Don't let the boat heel to leeward as you bear away around the buoy, this will make the boat want to turn upwind.
- Don't hit the buoy with the end of your boom as you let the sail out.
- Be aware of other boats around you.

2-boat length circle

Many rules refer to the 2-boat length circle, this is simply an imaginary circle around the buoy with a radius of 2 boat lengths.

2-boat lengths at windward mark

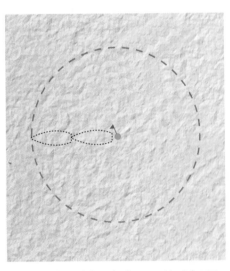

Most windward buoys are left to port, so it is advantageous to approach the buoy on starboard tack. Some boats will come towards the buoy on port tack and have to tack before going round the buoy. There is a rule that restricts what these boats may do, to reduce the risk of collisions.

No boat approaching on port and tacking inside the two boat length circle may cause a boat on starboard to have to luff (turn upwind) beyond a close hauled course. Any boat doing so must take a penalty.

If there are lots of boats on starboard tack coming towards the buoy it is safer for a port tack boat to tack outside the 2-boat length circle.

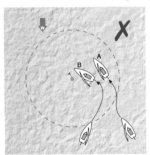

B forces A to luff above close hauled, and must take a penalty

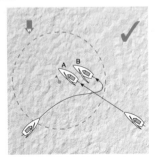

B should go behind A or slow her approach to arrive after A

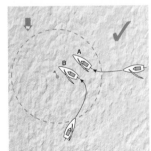

B may tack inside A, because A only has to luff to close hauled to avoid her

Reaching and Running

While you may steer straight between the off wind marks, try to stay in the strongest wind by sailing low in the gusts and high in lighter breeze.

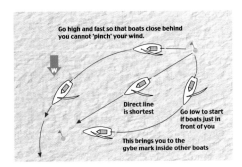

Go high and fast so that boats close behind you cannot 'pinch' your wind.

Direct line is shortest

Go low to start if boats just in front of you

This brings you to the gybe mark inside other boats

Running

When running straight downwind, be aware of boats behind you. Because the wind reaches them first, it is disturbed and slower by the time it reaches you, resulting in the boats behind catching you up. It is better to sail to one side or the other of boats behind you.

At an off wind mark

2-boat lengths at an off wind mark

When arriving at an offwind buoy, close to another boat, the racing rules dictate whether you are entitled to pass between the other boat and the buoy.

When the first boat enters the 2-boat length circle, the inner boat is only entitled to room if there is an overlap. If so, the outer boat must allow sufficient room for the inner boat to pass, allowing for a gybe if necessary. If there is no overlap, at the moment the first boat enters the circle, the inner boat must go round the buoy behind the outer boat.

Luffing Rights

You may wish to stop a boat overtaking to windward. To do this you may luff above your course to the next buoy, but the overtaking boat must have time to respond. You may not luff beyond head to wind. The overtaking boat must keep clear to windward of you unless it gets clear ahead. If it does you must immediately return to your original course.

Don't luff unless you're sure it's worth the lost time - this tactic often costs places in the race.

TOP TIP - To decide if you are in another boat's dirty wind, look to see if their burgee is pointing at you. If it is then you are probably being slowed down.

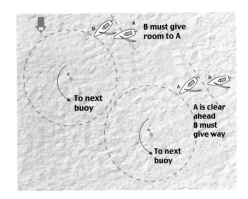

B must give room to A

To next buoy

A is clear ahead B must give way

To next buoy

TOP TIP - A little water in the boat can slow it significantly. If the crew is not hiking or trapezing, the reach or run can be a good time to empty the boat.

Leeward Buoy, Last Beat And Finish

Wide in, tight out

When passing the leeward buoy sail as close to it as possible as you start the beat. You should only turn as fast as you can sheet in. Go in quite wide. A wide approach will enable you to sail very close to the mark as you leave. To help the boat luff up, a small amount of leeward heel is useful. A overtakes B.

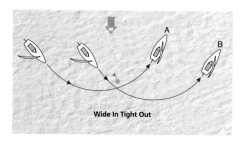

Wide In Tight Out

Last beat, consolidate and cover

By the time you reach the last beat, the boats will probably be quite spread out.

The priority is to consolidate your position by not letting any boats past you. To reduce the chance of this happening, stay between the boats behind you and the finish line to ensure they don't receive any beneficial wind changes that you miss.

If there is a boat quite near, try to stay directly upwind of it so it is in your dirty wind. A covers B.

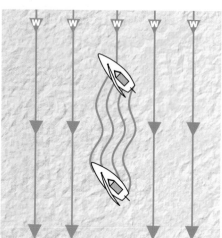

TOP TIP - As you arrive at the leeward buoy, work out if there is any flow of water with you or against you. If it is against you, leave the boat set up for going downwind, including the spinnaker, until the last possible moment. If it is with you, drop early and set up for the beat to windward before rounding.

Finish line

One end of the finish line may be to leeward of the other. Try and judge this and go for the end that is nearest to you - the downwind end.

If you go beyond the lay line for the finish and there are other boats around you, you are allowed to hail for room to cross the finish line. A is given room despite being windward boat.

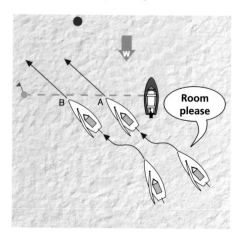

Room please

Why Do We Need The Rules?

The rules allow fair racing and should prevent collisions.
The majority of situations are covered by just a few rules. It is not necessary to understand them all when you start racing, a better understanding will come with experience. Be aware of your rights and obligations to others.

Penalties
Having broken a rule you can exonerate yourself by doing a penalty turn at the first opportunity.

A penalty turn will normally be one turn or two turns as defined by the rules. A one turn penalty is a tack and a gybe in the same continuous direction. A two turn penalty is 2 tacks and 2 gybes taken continuously in the same direction. Find out what penalties are in place before you race.

Protests
If somebody breaks a rule but does not do their penalty turns then you may **protest**. Inform the other boat that you intend to protest by calling "Protest". If they still do not take a penalty you should inform the race officer of your protest at the end of the race and complete a protest form. In order to help in the resolution of rules disputes in a more immediate, accessible and appropriate way, the RYA Racing Charter encourages the use of Advisory Hearings (no penalty) or RYA Arbitration(reduced penalty) as an alternative to a formal protest hearing where possible disqualification may be the outcome.

Choosing a Boat

When you start racing consider what is the right boat for you. You should consider:

- How big you are
- What sort of water you will be sailing on
- What dinghies are already sailed there
- How experienced you are
- How difficult is the dinghy to sail

When Boats Meet

When boats are on opposite tacks, a port-tack boat shall keep clear of a starboard-tack boat

When boats are on the same tack and overlapped, a windward boat shall keep clear of a leeward boat

When boats are on the same tack and not overlapped, a boat clear astern shall keep clear of a boat clear ahead.

DVD Boat Preparation For Racing

You do not need a brand new boat and sails to do well but some simple preparation will help:

- Make sure your boat is clean and has no big scatches or dents
- Check that all the controls work
- Ensure the mast is in the same place, and at the same angle, as the fast boats in your class - check the tuning guide on the class website
- Make sure the dinghy is as light as possible (most classes have a minimum weight)

Insurance, Certificates, Memberships

Before you start racing you will need third party insurance cover for your dinghy.

Many classes require a Measurement Certificate, this means that the boat has been measured, weighed and possibly buoyancy tested to conform with class rules.

It is also a good idea to join your class association. They are a good source of information and organise class events and training days. The class website is an excellent place to start.

8 | Performance Sailing

This chapter is about understanding the forces on the boat: how to use them in light winds and neutralise them in strong winds.

In order to understand the forces on a boat, practise experimenting with them. Start by immobilising the rudder, by very loosely securing it to the centreline of the boat with a strong piece of elastic. This will allow you to regain control again quickly if necessary. Try this in light winds to start with, on a quiet safe piece of water, in a dinghy with a jib (with or without a crew).

Firstly, it is important to understand how the boat behaves if it is heeled towards the wind or away from the wind.

Secondly, learn what happens if you sheet in the jib and ease the mainsail and vice versa.

By heeling the boat to leeward and/or sheeting in the mainsail you can turn the boat into the wind. Similarly, by heeling the boat on top of yourself and/or sheeting in the jib you can make the boat bear away.

As a short exercise, see if you can sail your boat on a beam reach by using these forces. Change one variable at a time initially.

The same rules apply to catamarans but the response is slower because there are two hulls and rudders. The effect of sail control on the boat is therefore less direct.

Once you have mastered sailing on a beam reach, try sailing around a triangular course using all the points of sailing.

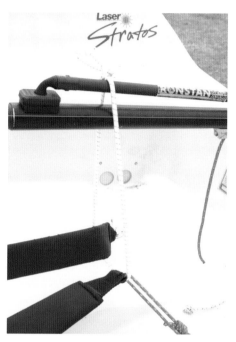

To bear away, ease main sheet and heel to windward

TOP TIP - When sailing without using the rudder, raise the centreboard one third. This reduces the heeling and turning forces by raising the centre of lateral resistance and moving it back.

To luff, ease jib sheet and heel to leeward

🔵DVD Sailing Upwind

Tell tales

The sails are sheeted in when sailing upwind. There are two basic ways to understand your performance. There is mechanical feedback from items such as tell tales, compass, burgees, and the front of the sail. There is also a more intuitive response, where you sense the 'feel' of the boat. The best option is to combine the two.

When sailing upwind, there are a number of variables:

- wind direction
- balance (your ability to hike or trapeze)
- steering a course
- sail setting (which will be fairly static)
- centreboard, which will be fully down
- trim (which will be forward to stop transom drag)
- created apparent wind due to speed (catamarans)

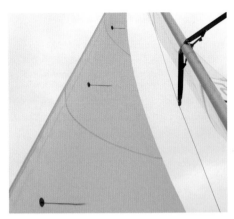

With perfect jib set-up, windward tell tales stream slightly upwards

> TOP TIP - Never focus on the leeward tell tales when sailing to windward, as you will be many degrees off the wind before it moves.

When learning, the tell tales are very important to give you feedback on steering. Keep looking to see how high you are pointing by luffing the boat slightly and checking the tell tales. At the perfect angle to the wind, the windward tell tales will stream slightly upwards.

Intuition

In certain conditions, ie wet tell-tales sticking to the sail, feedback may be poor or non-existent, so try to develop an intuitive feel:

- Sail with your eyes shut for short periods
- Look out for gusts, for example indicated by dark patches on water
- Play with the sail controls and get feedback from your crew on how your steering is affected

Once you are fully hiked (and balanced), only steering and sail-setting will vary. If the jib is in its correct beating position for the wind strength, the only variables will be the steering and the mainsheet. The helm must concentrate fully on steering whilst the crew looks for gusts, windshifts and traffic. (See page 31 in Sailing with Spinnakers on holding the tiller extension and steering).

If you wander away from the wind, the sails will generate MORE power than if fully close hauled. This will result in having to ease the mainsheet to lose power. If instead you concentrate on pointing as close to the wind as possible (tell tales) you will be able to handle the power without playing the mainsheet as much.

> GOLDE RULE - Specific set-up varies from class to class, so consult your class association. It does make a massive difference. Mast rake is used as the primary means of powering up or de-powering most dinghy and catamaran rigs.

Sailing Downwind – Reaching and Running

When using tell tales on the jib reaching downwind, sheet the sail until the windward tell tale collapses. Now ease until the leeward tell tale collapses. This will give you an idea of the sheeting 'band', within which you need to operate. Note that the upper tell tales will collapse first. As on a reach, exert a downward pressure on the sheet to control the leech. The jib cars can therefore be moved forward or out.

When running exactly downwind without a spinnaker, it normally pays to sheet the jib on the opposite side to the mainsail. This prevents it being blanketed by the mainsail and is known as goose-winging. Tell tales are not particularly helpful whilst running.

> TOP TIP – If in doubt always check the wind position by steering INTO the wind.

 Rig Controls

- The sheet varies the angle of the sail to the wind. In light winds, it tensions the jib leech according to the jib car position on the track.

- The kicker maintains mainsail twist, bends the mast and tensions the leech. Excessive amounts of kicker flattens the sail.

- The Cunningham compresses the mast, moves power forward in the mainsail and opens (eases) the leech.

- The outhaul flattens the lower part of the mainsail.

Jib car alters angle of sheet to vertical and therefore tensions leech or foot of jib.

Correct set-up for medium winds with little twist.

Open leech due to insufficient kicker tension.

Hooked leech due to excessive kicker tension.

On catamarans, the mainsail downhaul replaces the Cunningham. Mainsail shape, mast bend and rotation, and leech tension are all controlled by mainsheet tension and traveller position.

(DVD) Speed and Boat Handling

Light Winds

If you are sailing a two person boat, the light wind band varies from drifting conditions where the crew sits to leeward, through to the crew being on the windward side, but not hiking. In this wind band, which will vary according to your boat, concentrate on low drag, twisted sails and smooth movement with an emphasis on trim.

To check the trim, simply look at the transom drag, if it looks turbulent move forward. This is particularly important in the new designs with very flat **rocker**.

Balance the boat with a small amount of leeward heel. This gives the rudder 'feel', the boat tries to turn into the wind and will help the sails to set better. Do not overdo this - too much rudder to correct this weather helm will cause turbulence and slow the boat down. The rudder will then act as a brake trying to resist the turning moment. You may have more control holding the tiller pan-handle style.

1 Boat heeled to leeward (balance)

2 Weight right forward (trim), transom clear of water

3 Centre board down

4 Mast upright for maximum power

5 Kicker slack, sail twisted to set for stronger breeze higher up

6 No Cunningham - creases left in sail

7 Outhaul tight

8 Sail flat to increase air flow

9 Leech tell tales streaming

10 Windward jib tell tales just lifting with jib cars back

TOP TIP - Sheet in to point higher. If over-sheeted, the sail stalls, resulting in poor pointing and speed. IF IN DOUBT EASE THE SHEET.

Roll tacks

In light winds, try to take advantage of gusts and wind shifts. You may find yourself tacking more often, which slows the boat, so use **roll tacks**. In roll tacking, the crew weight and the forces on the boat are used to your advantage, resulting in more efficient performance. The rudder resistance is reduced as the rudder is being used less to turn the boat. Roll tacks reduce the drag and deceleration caused as the boat turns upright and the sails flap, generating air resistance.

By rolling the boat with your body weight, the sails are fanned through the air, keeping them filled for longer and dragging less. In this way the air flow is re-attached to the sail quicker after the tack.

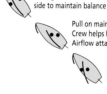
Crew goes back to leeward side to maintain balance

Pull on mainsail.
Crew helps helm pull boat upright.
Airflow attaches and boat accelerates.

Boat ready to sail on new tack.
Mainsail out.

Boat head to wind, crew join
Rig and hull turn onto new t
Boat heeled into turn.

Use mainsheet tension, rudder and heel to turn boat

Crew to leeward.
Small amount of heel.
Discuss tack.

Step 1

Step 2

Step 3

Step 4

Step 1 Check the area is clear. Gently steer the boat up head to wind, by allowing the forces created by the leeward heel and some tiller angle, to turn the boat. The crew joins the helm on the windward side to flick the mast and sails past head-to-wind.

Step 2 As the sails collapse, cross the boat, sheet the jib across and ease the main. The forces on the rig help swing the bow away from the wind and onto the new close hauled course.

Step 3 The boat is pointing in the correct direction but will have excess leeward heel.

Step 4 The helm and possibly the crew now move smoothly to windward while pulling in the sails, thus accelerating the boat back to its entry speed (in racing, more than its entry speed is illegal). The crew may now need to return to their leeward position.

The effectiveness of roll tacking will vary from boat to boat. The Enterprise is a near perfect roll tacking design. Roll tacking is not quite so effective with catamarans but by moving crew weight to the windward **quarter** (the back corner) and spinning the boat on the inside hull as you enter the no-go zone, the boat will turn more quickly.

TOP TIP - If your tacks are too flat, delay the crew joining the helm by a second. You will only generate maximum roll past head to wind.

(DVD) Roll gybes

The same forces can be used to gybe the boat, with windward heel initiating the turn. Do not force the mainsail over, more assist it in its natural progress as again, the forces on the boat and sails will be neutral. Smooth movement is the key. This manoeuvre can be used on dinghies, single-handers or with spinnakers.

Roll tacks and gybes can be used as the wind strength increases until you think that the forces are becoming too great to control. For example, you may have problems pulling the boat up again, having rolled the boat into the tack or gybe, so reduce the heel until you are tacking or gybing perfectly flat in strong winds.

Step 1

Step 2

Step 3

Step 4

Step 1 Preparation: check the area is clear and the boom is clear of the shroud.

Step 2 Roll the boat to windward to assist bearing away, mainsheet hand grasping the **falls** directly off the boom.

Step 3 Gybe the main positively as the leech starts to lift. Centralise the tiller if necessary and cross the boat smartly to balance.

Step 4 Balance the boat, sheet sails correctly and keep a good look out.

TOP TIP
Footwork is crucial when tacking or gybing. Move your feet across the boat only when you yourself have to move across. Premature or defensive footwork causes capsizes.

Many people gybe quite crudely by simply standing up and pulling the tiller to windward, crossing the boat and centralising the tiller as the sail comes over. Skiff-style boats are better handled by continuously adjusting the tiller as the boat turns, only making a large tiller adjustment if balance becomes a problem.

Light To Medium Winds

This wind band starts with the crew sitting on the windward side but not hiking and ends with the crew fully hiked with the rig at maximum power.

In this wind band we are searching for power to get the crew hiking or on the trapeze. Again, do not use the kicking strap as this bends the mast and de-powers the sails. Likewise, do not use the Cunningham to remove creases in the sail, as this will again bend the mast through compression and ease the upper leech, resulting in less pointing. Simply use the main and jib sheet to control the leech tension and hence pointing. Just as in light winds, if the boat feels stalled and seems to be slow, try easing the sheet. Jib cars will start to ease forward from the very light winds to exert more tension on the leech of the jib.

As in very light winds, the centreboard will be adjusted for the point of sail and balance will be very important. Trim may be less important, but still check the transom for drag.

1   Boat level (balance), crew fully hiked

2   Weight forward (trim)

3   Centre board down

4   Mast straight for maximum power, rake basically upright - see class tuning guide

5   Take slack out of kicker but do not tension. Small amount of mainsail twist

6   No Cunningham - creases left in sail

7   Outhaul eased for maximum power

8   Sail full for maximum power

9   In general, leech tell tales just streaming

10 Windward jib tell tales just lifting with jib cars forward a little

Strong Winds

The sails develop excessive power but once you have already exerted your maximum balance by hiking or trapezing fully, it is necessary to de-power. The trick is to sail the boat flat, easing the sails in the gusts and sheeting in for the lulls. Tension the kicker to control the leech twist as you play the mainsheet. This is because if the boom rises as you ease the mainsheet, the sail will develop more power which will heel the boat further. Jib sheet cars can move aft again, reducing the tension on the leech, increasing the tension on the foot and aiding twist and de-powering of the jib. The Cunningham can finally be used, as it will compress and bend the mast, flatten the sail and twist open the leech in the upper part of the sail.

Upwind, balance combined with speed will be a key factor. If the boat slows then the forces (heel) will build very quickly and the boat will simply fall over while going very slowly. Keep easing sails to maintain some speed through the water, even if this hinders pointing. In moderate gusts you can get away with just easing the mainsail, but in the bigger gusts ease the jib sheet otherwise the jib slot will choke as you are playing so much mainsheet.

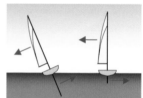

Raise the centreboard to reduce the forces below the boat (lateral resistance). This also raises them closer to the rig, reducing heeling.

Once sailing downwind, the forces will be handled by steering; the lower you sail, the less the heeling force on the boat. Trim well back to counteract the forward forces on the rig.

On catamarans, try to flatten the sail. Increase downhaul and mainsheet tension and play the traveller. Open the jib slot by moving the jib cars back or out.

1   Boat balanced, crew fully hiked

2   Weight forward but adjusted to allow bow to rise in waves (trim)

3   Centre board partly raised to ease heeling

4   Mast raked back to reduce power

5   Full kicker tension to bend mast and flatten sail

6   Full Cunningham to flatten sail, twisting top half open and bringing power forward in mainsail

7   Outhaul tight to depower (less tight in waves)

8   Sail flat to reduce power

9   Leech tell tales streaming

10 Luff tell tales just streaming with jib cars further back

Class Set-Up

Specific set-up makes a big difference and varies from class to class, so consult your class association. Rake is used as a primary means of powering up or de-powering most rigs.

Wind Shifts

The wind is rarely steady; constantly changing in strength and direction. For further information consult the chapter on Day Sailing. Studying the wind is a life-long pursuit. Aim to be in the best position, sailing as fast as possible. The wind gives you the opportunity to do both these things, so understanding and observation will be key. When sailing downwind, gusts give more speed and a lower course. Sailing upwind, gusts can be an advantage to increase speed, but more importantly, shifts allow the greatest gain. In order to position yourself correctly you must differentiate between an oscillating shift and a persistent shift.

An oscillating shift moves in a series of shifts about a mean direction, while a persistent shift (such as a sea breeze) moves in one general direction (although it may oscillate as it goes in this direction).

For the persistent shift, one side of the course will give a gain over the other side. For oscillating shifts, sailors who tack onto the favoured lifted shift every time will make a gain.

It is important to identify whether a shift is oscillating or persistent, as they each require a different reaction.

If you are lifted in an oscillating shift, stay on that tack as you are lifted. If you are lifted in a persistent shift, you will probably need to tack as the strategy will be to get to the inside of the bend. In order to do this, the earlier you take the headed course, the quicker you will get the gain from the long term lift. See Start Racing for further information.

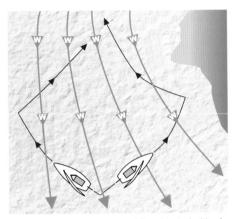

For a wind bend or a persistent shift, sail to the inside of the bend

TOP TIP
If racing remember you have to go around marks tacking on EVERY shift may not allow us to arrive at the mark.

TOP TIP
In light winds, sail in the strongest breeze regardless of direction.
In medium and strong winds, go for wind direction not strength.

Tides

As dinghies sail relatively slowly, tide can be a key factor and make a crucial difference to your performance. See page 23 in Day Sailing for more details. Your strategy will depend upon the strength of the tidal flow.

Look out for headlands, shorelines and the opportunity to escape, or use, tidal flow to your advantage. Study tide tables and a tidal stream atlas before departure to see how much impact it will have on your sailing in the predicted wind.

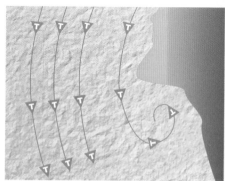

Tide flows around headland

Waves

Particularly if sailing on the sea or large inland water, you will rarely have flat water. To use the waves, use body movement (balance), steering and trim to harness or cancel the extra force of waves.

When the boat is lifted by a wave, it is exposed to stronger, cleaner breeze and is likely to heel.

Sailing upwind, you will generally need to de-power the boat as you are raised into the stronger breeze. Steer up the face of the wave and bear away down the back face of the wave. You may need to ease the mainsail slightly on the top of the wave and pull it back on as you sail down the back of the wave.

Downwind conditions are more in your favour. Instead of shedding power as the boat is picked up by the wave, encourage the boat to surf down the face.

Trim forward with body weight and pump the jib and mainsheet to promote surfing. Once surfing, continue to trim to the new apparent wind on the sails. Move down the face of the wave trying to gain as much distance to leeward as possible without falling off the face. If your bow is about to rise into the back of the next wave in front, steer either way to prevent this and trim the sails to suit. Move back to help the bow to rise.

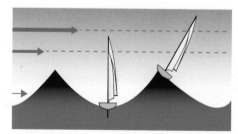

TOP TIP
In waves, always try to sail with the bow pointing slightly down the wave.

9 | Glossary of Nautical Terms

Apparent wind Direction and speed of wind, affected by course and speed of boat

Back (verb) (1) Rotate anti-clockwise, or against the sun

Backed (2) A sail filled in reverse to the normal direction by the wind

Balance How level the boat is

Bias Angle of start line to wind if not 90°

Blanketing Sheltering one sail behind another

Buoy Floating mark used for navigation or mooring

Burgee Small flag at top of mast

Centreboard Hinged plate used to resist sideways movement (leeway)

Cleat Device for securing a rope

C.O.G. Course over the ground

Cunningham Line for tensioning leading edge of sail (downhaul)

Dagger board Plate used to resist leeway, inserted vertically not hinged (see centreboard)

Deviation Deflection of compass needle by other magnetic materials

Downhaul See Cunningham

Falls Rope hanging free after passing through block eg mainsheet falls

Fully Battened Sails with full width battens, from luff to leech

Gradient Wind Wind due to weather systems, not local effects

Gybe (verb) To turn the boat so that the wind blows from the opposite side, going downwind

Halyard Rope or wire used to raise sails and to tension leading edge

Header Wind shift taking you further from your upwind objective

Heeling Leaning over

Kicker Rope or wire used to control twist in mainsail

Larks Foot Rope looped through itself

Lay Line Imaginary line along which one can sail to windward mark without tacking

Leech Back edge of sail

Leeward The side of the boat that the wind is blowing away from, ie the downwind side

Leeway Sideways drift of boat due to wind pressure

Lift Wind shift taking you closer to your upwind objective

Luff (verb) To turn the boat towards the wind

Luff (noun) Leading edge of sail

Mast Rake Angle of mast to vertical

Mooring buoy Buoy used to park boat

Neap tide Period in month when tidal range is smallest

Outhaul Line used to tension foot of sail horizontally

Planing Skimming over surface of water on bow wave

Rocker Amount of curve in bottom of boat

Sheet Rope used to control angle of sail to wind

Spinnaker Balloon shaped sail used downwind

Spring tides Period in month when tidal range is greatest

Tack (noun) The side of the boat opposite the boom, usually the side the wind is coming from, ie port tack or starboard tack

Tack (verb) Turning the boat so that the wind blows from the opposite side, facing upwind

Tell Tale Wool or lightweight tape used to detect airflow

Tidal Range Difference between high and low water

Transit Two fixed objects in line

Trim Fore and aft adjustment of weight in the boat

Variation Difference in direction between grid and magnetic North

Veer (verb) Rotate clockwise or in the same direction as the sun. See 'back'

Warp Rope used for anchor or mooring

Waypoint Chart position input to GPS memory

Windward The side of the boat that the wind is blowing on to, ie the upwind side

10 RYA National Sailing Scheme

Following the basics of Levels 1 and 2, there is a choice of courses to enable you to pursue whichever part of the sport you wish. All the courses can be taken in a minimum of two days, in keelboats, dinghies or multihulls.

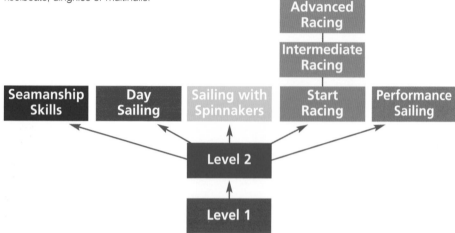

Level 1 Start Sailing
An introduction to the sport, covering the minimum knowledge required to get afloat under supervision.

Level 2 Basic Skills
Becoming a competent sailor in light winds.

Seamanship Skills
How to handle the boat in all circumstances and solve problems afloat.

Day Sailing
Passage planning and decision making for small boat cruising.

Sailing with Spinnakers
Everything you need to know to sail modern three-sail boats.

Start Racing
The start line for enjoying club racing. All you need to know to get round the course.

Intermediate Racing
Develop and improve your racing techniques and knowledge for club racing.

Advanced Racing
Develop your racing skills and knowledge for open meetings and regattas.

Performance Sailing
Improve your boat handling and confidence in performance boats.

Further Reading

Most of these publications are available on the RYA website: www.rya.org.uk Order hotline: **0845 345 0372**

Start Sailing The Beginners Handbook
RYA G3

RYA National Sailing Scheme Syllabus and Logbook
RYA G4

RYA Handy Guide to Racing Rules
RYA YR7

RYA Racing Rules of Sailing
RYA YR1

Start Sailing
(video & DVD), RYA

Better Sailing
(video & DVD), RYA

RYA Knots Splices & Ropework
by Gordon Perry & Steve Judkins, RYA G63

Index

Index

Index